ألف ليلة وليلة

لمتعلمي اللغة العربية المبتدئين

One Thousand and One Nights

for Elementary Arabic Language Learners

lingualism

© 2023 by Matthew Aldrich

The author's moral rights have been asserted. All rights reserved. No part of this document may be reproduced or transmitted in any form or by any means, electronic, mechanical, photocopying, recording, or otherwise, without prior written permission of the publisher.

ISBN: 978-1-949650-91-4

Conceptualized by Matthew Aldrich

Written by Ahmad Al-Masri

Edited by Hend Khaled and Matthew Aldrich

Illustrations by Duc-Minh Vu

Audio by Mohamed Shehata

website: www.lingualism.com

email: contact@lingualism.com

Table of Contents

II .... INTRODUCTION

V .... HOW TO USE THIS BOOK

1 .... الفَصْلُ الأَوَّلُ: الوَزيرُ وَابْنَتُهُ وَالمَلِكُ
Chapter 1: The Vizier, His Daughter, and the King

8 .... الفَصْلُ الثّاني: الجِنِّيُّ وَالتّاجِرُ
Chapter 2: The Genie and the Merchant

17 .... الفَصْلُ الثّالِثُ: الصَّيّادُ وَالسَّمَكَةُ الذَّهَبِيَّةُ
Chapter 3: The Fisherman and the Golden Fish

25 .... الفَصْلُ الرّابِعُ: عَلاءُ الدّينِ وَالمِصْباحُ السِّحْرِيُّ
Chapter 4: Aladdin and the Magic Lamp

34 .... الفَصْلُ الخامِسُ: عَلي بابا وَالأَرْبَعونَ لِصًّا
Chapter 5: Ali Baba and the Forty Thieves

41 .... الفَصْلُ السّادِسُ: الفَلّاحُ الذَّكِيُّ وَالجِنِّيُّ المُشاغِبُ
Chapter 6: The Clever Farmer and the Mischievous Genie

49 .... الفَصْلُ السّابِعُ: لِصُّ الإِسْكَنْدَرِيَّةِ وَرَئيسُ الشُّرْطَةِ
Chapter 7: The Thief of Alexandria and the Police Chief

57 .... الفَصْلُ الثّامِنُ: الطّائِرُ الأَزْرَقُ
Chapter 8: The Blue Bird

65 .... الفَصْلُ التّاسِعُ: الفَتاةُ وَالعَجوزُ السِّحْرِيَّةُ
Chapter 9: The Girl and the Magical Old Woman

72 .... الفَصْلُ العاشِرُ: الأَميرُ وَالتِّنّينُ
Chapter 10: The Prince and the Dragon

Introduction

"**One Thousand and One Nights for Elementary Arabic Language Learners**" is a captivating anthology designed specifically for adult Arabic language learners at the elementary level. This unique collection features the cherished classic tales in a simplified, yet engaging format, making it an excellent resource for those venturing into the enchanting world of Arabic language and literature.

The book comes with an array of special features to ensure an immersive and effective learning experience:

- **Diacritics for Pronunciation:** We've included diacritical marks (tashkeel) in the Arabic text to assist you in correct pronunciation, and to clarify the meaning of the words, easing your reading experience.

- **Professional Audio Accompaniment:** The book is supplemented with high-quality, slow-paced audio readings by a professional voice artist who is a native Arabic speaker. This allows you to listen and mimic the correct pronunciation, intonation, and rhythm of the Arabic language.

- **Comprehension Questions and Answers:** Each chapter is followed by a set of comprehension questions, along with their answers. This interactive feature helps to reinforce your understanding of the story and the language constructs used within it.

- **English Translations:** To support your learning, we've provided English translations of the stories. These can be used as a reference to cross-check your understanding of the Arabic text.

All these features work together to provide a comprehensive and enriching learning experience, ensuring you make consistent progress in your Arabic language journey.

The tales in this book have been carefully curated and reimagined to match the language proficiency of elementary-level learners. We have incorporated level-appropriate vocabulary throughout the stories, ensuring you are neither overwhelmed by complexity nor left unchallenged. To enhance memorization and recognition, we've deliberately woven repetitive patterns of phrases and language structures into the text, encouraging natural language acquisition and recall.

Each chapter is short, and perfectly crafted to be absorbed in a single sitting, allowing you to steadily build your comprehension skills and vocabulary without feeling rushed. The stories retain the intrigue and charm of the original tales, providing you with a sense of accomplishment and enjoyment as you navigate your way through each tale.

Once you've mastered the stories and vocabulary in this book, we invite you to progress to the "One Thousand and One Nights for Intermediate Arabic Language Learners". In this next step of your language journey, you'll find the same beloved stories, but presented in slightly different versions. These alternate renditions are imbued with greater detail, building on the vocabulary you learn in this book, and introducing you to new vocabulary and more nuanced language structures. This ensures a smooth, seamless transition towards more advanced language learning.

With "One Thousand and One Nights for Elementary Arabic Language Learners", not only will you embark on a remarkable journey through some of the most enchanting stories ever told, but you'll also be laying a strong and solid foundation for your Arabic language learning adventure.

How to Use This Book

"One Thousand and One Nights for Elementary Arabic Language Learners" has been designed to offer flexibility to adapt to your individual learning style. Here's how you can utilize the features of the book according to your needs:

1. **Choose Your Approach:** You have the freedom to approach the stories in multiple ways. You could begin by tackling the Arabic text first, immersing yourself in the structure of the language and the flow of the story. Alternatively, you could start by listening to the accompanying audio, to attune your ear to the sound and rhythm of Arabic. This can be particularly helpful if you are a more auditory learner.

2. **Use English Translations:** If you're finding the Arabic text or audio challenging, you can refer to the English translations to aid your understanding. Over time, as your comprehension improves, you could challenge yourself by attempting to read or listen to the Arabic without relying on the translations.

3. **Engage with Questions:** You can choose to tackle the comprehension questions before or after reading the story. Attempting them beforehand can provide a focus for your reading, while answering them after allows you to assess your understanding of the text.

Remember, the answers provided in the book are examples and your own answers, while differently worded, may still be correct.

4. **Repetition and Practice:** This book has been designed to promote repetition and practice, key strategies for language learning. We encourage you to revisit chapters and listen to the audio multiple times to reinforce your understanding and memorization.

Remember, the most effective learning strategy is the one that works best for you. So don't be afraid to experiment with different approaches until you find what suits you best.

Visit <u>www.lingualism.com/audio</u>, where you can find the free accompanying audio to download or stream (at variable playback rates).

الفَصْلُ الأَوَّلُ
الوَزيرُ وَابْنَتُهُ وَالمَلِكُ

في يَوْمٍ مِنَ الأَيّامِ، في بِلادٍ بَعيدَةٍ، كانَ هُناكَ مَلِكٌ حَكيمٌ وَعادِلٌ يُدْعى شَهْرَيارَ. كانَ يَحْكُمُ مَمْلَكَةً كَبيرَةً، وَكانَ مَحبوبًا مِنْ شَعْبِهِ.

في مَحْكَمَةِ المَلِكِ، كانَ هُناكَ رَجُلٌ حَكيمٌ يُدْعى جَعْفَرًا وَكانَ هُوَ الوَزيرُ. كانَ يُساعِدُ المَلِكَ في اتِّخاذِ القَراراتِ المُهِمَّةِ. كانَ جَعْفَرٌ

رَجُلًا طَيِّبًا وَمُخْلِصًا، وَكَانَتْ لَدَيْهِ ابْنَةٌ جَمِيلَةٌ تُدْعى شَهْرَزَادَ.

كَانَتْ شَهْرَزَادُ فَتَاةً ذَكِيَّةً وَشُجَاعَةً. كَانَتْ تُحِبُّ القِرَاءَةَ وَالتَّعَلُّمَ عَنِ العَالَمِ. كَانَتْ تَعْرِفُ العَدِيدَ مِنَ القِصَصِ وَتَسْتَطِيعُ سَرْدَهَا بِطَرِيقَةٍ تَجْعَلُ النَّاسَ يَسْتَمِعُونَ.

فِي أَحَدِ الأَيَّامِ، قَرَّرَ المَلِكُ شَهْرَيَارُ أَنَّهُ يَحْتَاجُ إِلَى مَلِكَةٍ. طَلَبَ مِنْ وَزِيرِهِ أَنْ يَجِدَ لَهُ زَوْجَةً. بَحَثَ جَعْفَرُ لِفَتْرَةٍ طَوِيلَةٍ وَلَكِنَّهُ لَمْ يَتَمَكَّنْ مِنْ إِيجَادِ زَوْجَةٍ مُنَاسِبَةٍ لِلْمَلِكِ.

خَطَرَتْ لِشَهْرَزَادَ فِكْرَةٌ. ذَهَبَتْ إِلَى وَالِدِهَا الوَزِيرِ وَقَالَتْ: "أَبِي، أُرِيدُ أَنْ أَكُونَ زَوْجَةَ المَلِكِ. لَدَيَّ العَدِيدُ مِنَ القِصَصِ لِأَرْوِيَهَا لَهُ. يُمْكِنُنِي أَنْ أَجْعَلَهُ سَعِيدًا."

كَانَ الوَزِيرُ قَلِقًا بِشَأْنِ ابْنَتِهِ. كَانَ يَعْرِفُ أَنَّ المَلِكَ شَهْرَيَارَ يُمْكِنُ أَنْ يَغْضَبَ كَثِيرًا أَحْيَانًا. لَكِنَّ شَهْرَزَادَ كَانَتْ عَازِمَةً عَلَى الزَّوَاجِ مِنَ المَلِكِ.

وَبِالتَّالي وافَقَ الوَزيرُ عَلى الزَّواجِ. أَخْبَرَ المَلِكَ شَهْرَيارَ عَنِ ابْنَتِهِ، وَوافَقَ المَلِكُ عَلى الزَّواجِ مِنها.

في لَيْلَةِ زِفافِهِما، بَدَأَتْ شَهْرَزادُ تَروي لِلْمَلِكِ قِصَّةً. كانَتِ القِصَّةُ مُثيرَةً لِلاهْتِمامِ لِدَرَجَةِ أَنَّ المَلِكَ أرادَ سَماعَ المَزيدِ مِنها. فَقالَتْ شَهْرَزادُ: "سَأُكْمِلُ القِصَّةَ لَيْلَةَ الغَدِ إذا سَمَحْتَ لي." فَوافَقَ المَلِكُ شَهْرَيارُ عَلى طَلَبِها وَأَرادَ سَماعَ المَزيدِ مِنَ القِصَصِ.

وَهَكَذا بَدَأَتْ شَهْرَزادُ في سَرْدِ القِصَصِ لِلْمَلِكِ شَهْرَيارَ كُلَّ لَيْلَةٍ. كانَتِ القِصَصُ مَليئَةً بِالمُغامَراتِ وَالغُموضِ وَالحُبِّ. كانَ المَلِكُ مُتَشَوِّقًا لِسَماعِ كُلِّ قِصَّةٍ جَديدَةٍ وَكانَ يَتَعَلَّمُ مِنها الكَثيرَ عَنِ الحَياةِ وَالعالَمِ.

Questions

1. ما هُوَ اسْمُ المَلِكِ الحَكيمِ العادِلِ؟

2. ماذا كانَتْ شَهْرَزادُ تُحِبُّ أَنْ تَفْعَلَ؟

3. ماذا طَلَبَ المَلِكُ شَهْرَيارُ مِنْ وَزيرِهِ جَعْفَرٍ؟

4. كَيْفَ تَعَرَّفَتْ شَهْرَزادُ عَلى المَلِكِ شَهْرَيارَ؟

5. ماذا بَدَأَتْ شَهْرَزادُ تَفْعَلُ كُلَّ لَيْلَةٍ بَعْدَ زَواجِها مِنَ المَلِكِ شَهْرَيارَ؟

Answers

1. اِسْمُ المَلِكِ هُوَ شَهْرَيارُ.

2. كانَتْ شَهْرَزادُ تُحِبُّ القِراءَةَ وَالتَّعَلُّمَ عَنِ العالَمِ، وَكانَتْ تَعْرِفُ العَديدَ مِنَ القِصَصِ وَتَسْتَطيعُ سَرْدَها.

3. طَلَبَ المَلِكُ شَهْرَيارُ مِنْ وَزيرِهِ جَعْفَرٍ أَنْ يَجِدَ لَهُ زَوْجَةً.

4. ذَهَبَتْ شَهْرَزادُ إِلى والِدِها الوَزيرِ وَقالَتْ إِنَّها تُريدُ أَنْ تَكونَ زَوْجَةَ المَلِكِ، وَبِالتّالي أَخْبَرَ الوَزيرُ المَلِكَ عَنِ ابْنَتِهِ، وَوافَقَ المَلِكُ عَلى الزَّواجِ مِنْها.

5. بَدَأَتْ شَهْرَزادُ تَرْوي قِصَصًا لِلْمَلِكِ شَهْرَيارَ كُلَّ لَيْلَةٍ.

Chapter 1: The Vizier, His Daughter, and the King

Once upon a time, in a faraway land, there was a wise and just king named Shahriyar. He ruled a great kingdom and was loved by his people.

In the king's court, there was a wise man named Ja'far, who was the vizier. He helped the king make important decisions. Ja'far was a kind and loyal man, and he had a beautiful daughter named Scheherazade.

Scheherazade was a intelligent, brave girl. She loved reading and learning about the world. She knew many stories and could tell them in a way that made people listen.

One day, King Shahriyar decided that he needed a queen. He asked his vizier to find him a wife. Ja'far searched for a long time but could not find a suitable wife for the king.

Scheherazade had an idea. She went to her father, the vizier, and said, "Father, I want to be the king's wife. I have many stories to tell him. I can make him happy."

The vizier was worried about his daughter. He knew that King Shahriyar could get very angry sometimes. But Scheherazade was determined to marry the king.

So the vizier agreed to the marriage. He told King Shahriyar about his daughter, and the king agreed to marry her.

On their wedding night, Scheherazade began to tell the king a story. The story was so interesting that the king wanted to hear more. Scheherazade said, "I will finish the story tomorrow night if you allow me." King Shahriyar agreed and wanted to hear more stories.

And so Scheherazade began to tell stories to King Shahriyar every night. The stories were full of adventures, mysteries, and love. The king was eager to hear every new story and learned a lot about life and the world from them.

Questions
1. What is the name of the wise and just king?
2. What did Scheherazade love to do?
3. What did King Shahriyar ask his vizier Ja'far to do?
4. How did Scheherazade meet King Shahriyar?
5. What did Scheherazade begin to do every night after marrying King Shahriyar?

Answers
1. The name of the king is Shahriyar.
2. Scheherazade loved reading and learning about the world, and she knew many stories that she could tell.
3. King Shahriyar asked his vizier Ja'far to find him a wife.
4. Scheherazade went to her father, the vizier, and said she wanted to be the king's wife, so the vizier told the king about his daughter, and the king agreed to marry her.
5. Scheherazade began to tell stories to King Shahriyar every night.

الفَصْلُ الثّاني
الجِنِّيُّ وَالتّاجِرُ

في اللَّيْلَةِ التّالِيَةِ، طَلَبَ المَلِكُ شَهْرَيارُ مِنْ شَهْرَزادَ أَنْ تَرْوِيَ لَهُ قِصَّةً جَديدَةً. فَبَدَأَتْ شَهْرَزادُ بِسَرْدِ قِصَّةِ التّاجِرِ وَالجِنِّيِّ العَجيبِ.

ذاتَ يَوْمٍ، ذَهَبَ تاجِرٌ غَنِيٌّ في رِحْلَةٍ بَعيدَةٍ لِبَيْعِ بِضاعَتِهِ. بَعْدَ رِحْلَةٍ طَويلَةٍ وَمُتْعِبَةٍ، تَوَقَّفَ التّاجِرُ لِيَسْتَريحَ تَحْتَ شَجَرَةٍ. وَبَيْنَما

هُوَ جالِسٌ هُناكَ، ظَهَرَ جِنِّيٌّ عِمْلاقٌ وَغاضِبٌ.

قالَ الجِنِّيُّ لِلتّاجِرِ: "سَأَقْتُلُكَ لِأَنَّكَ قَدْ دَمَّرْتَ بَيْتي." كانَ التّاجِرُ مَذْعورًا وَلَمْ يَفْهَمْ ما يَقْصِدُهُ الجِنِّيُّ. طَلَبَ مِنَ الجِنِّيِّ أَنْ يَشْرَحَ لَهُ سَبَبَ غَضَبِهِ.

فَأَجابَ الجِنِّيُّ: "عِنْدَما جِئْتَ وَنَزَعْتَ هَذا الجِذْعَ الخَشَبِيَّ لِتَجْلِسَ عَلَيْهِ، سَقَطَتْ عَلَيَّ بَعْضُ الأَشْياءِ وَدَمَّرَتْ بَيْتي الصَّغيرَ الَّذي كُنْتُ أَعيشُ فيهِ."

كانَ التّاجِرُ حَزينًا لِما حَدَثَ، وَلَكِنَّهُ لَمْ يَكُنْ يَعْرِفُ أَنَّ هُناكَ بَيْتَ جِنِّيٍّ خَلْفَ الشَّجَرَةِ. طَلَبَ مِنَ الجِنِّيِّ أَنْ يَتَحَلَّى بِالرَّحْمَةِ وَيُسامِحَهُ.

قالَ الجِنِّيُّ: "سَأُعْطيكَ فُرْصَةً لِتَأْتِيَ بِشَخْصٍ يُقْنِعُني بِأَلّا أَقْتُلَكَ. إِذا فَشِلْتَ، فَسَأَقْتُلُكَ حَتْمًا."

ذَهَبَ التَّاجِرُ فِي رِحْلَةٍ طَوِيلَةٍ بَحْثًا عَنْ شَخْصٍ يُساعِدُهُ. وَفِي نِهايَةِ المَطافِ، وَجَدَ رَجُلًا عَجوزًا حَكيمًا كانَ يَعْرِفُ الكَثيرَ عَنِ الجِنِّ وَعالَمِهِمْ.

اِسْتَمَعَ الرَّجُلُ العَجوزُ لِقِصَّةِ التَّاجِرِ وَقَرَّرَ مُساعَدَتَهُ. ذَهَبا مَعًا إِلى مَكانِ الشَّجَرَةِ حَيْثُ كانَ الجِنِّيُّ يَنْتَظِرُهُمْ.

قالَ الرَّجُلُ العَجوزُ لِلْجِنِّيِّ: "أُريدُ أَنْ أَرْوِيَ لَكَ قِصَّةً قَبْلَ أَنْ تُقَرِّرَ مَصيرَ هَذا التَّاجِرِ. إِذا أَعْجَبَتْكَ القِصَّةُ، فَأَرْجو أَنْ تُسامِحَهُ وَتَتْرُكَهُ يَعيشُ."

وافَقَ الجِنِّيُّ عَلى سَماعِ القِصَّةِ. فَبَدَأَ الرَّجُلُ العَجوزُ يَروي قِصَّةً مُثيرَةً عَنِ المُغامَرَةِ وَالشَّجاعَةِ وَالتَّضْحِيَةِ. كانَتِ القِصَّةُ مَليئَةً بِالتَّشْويقِ وَالعِبَرِ الهامَّةِ.

بَعْدَ أَنْ سَمِعَ الجِنِّيُّ القِصَّةَ، قالَ: "لَقَدْ أَعْجَبَتْني القِصَّةُ كَثيرًا وَتَعَلَّمْتُ مِنها دُروسًا عَظيمَةً. سَأُسامِحُ التَّاجِرَ وَلَنْ أَقْتُلَهُ بِشَرْطِ أَنْ يَحْذَرَ مِنْ تَكْرارِ مِثْلِ هَذا الخَطَأِ مُسْتَقْبَلًا."

شَكَرَ التَّاجِرُ الجِنِّيَّ عَلى رَحْمَتِهِ وَوَعَدَ بِأَنْ يَكونَ حَذِرًا في تَصَرُّفاتِهِ. كَما شَكَرَ الرَّجُلَ العَجوزَ عَلى مُساعَدَتِهِ وَحِكْمَتِهِ. ثُمَّ عادَ التّاجِرُ إلى قَرْيَتِهِ وَأُسْرَتِهِ وَتَعَهَّدَ بِأَنْ يَكونَ أَكْثَرَ حَذَرًا وَعَطْفًا في تَعامُلِهِ مَعَ الطَّبيعَةِ وَكائِناتِها.

في اللَّيْلَةِ التّالِيَةِ، اِنْتَهَتْ شَهْرَزادُ مِنْ سَرْدِ قِصَّةِ التّاجِرِ وَالجِنِّيِّ. كانَ المَلِكُ شَهْرَيارُ مُنْبَهِرًا بِهَذِهِ القِصَّةِ وَأَرادَ سَماعَ المَزيدِ مِنَ القِصَصِ الرّائِعَةِ الَّتي تَرْويها شَهْرَزادُ. وَبِذَلِكَ، اِسْتَمَرَّتْ شَهْرَزادُ في سَرْدِ قِصَصِها لِلْمَلِكِ لَيْلَةً بَعْدَ لَيْلَةٍ، وَعَلَّمَتِ المَلِكَ وَشَعْبَهُ دُروسًا هامَّةً عَنِ الحَياةِ وَالحِكْمَةِ وَالعَدْلِ.

Questions

1. ما هِيَ القِصَّةُ الَّتي بَدَأَتْ شَهْرَزادُ تَرْويها في اللَّيْلَةِ الثّانِيَةِ؟

2. لِماذا غَضِبَ الجِنِّيُّ مِنَ التّاجِرِ؟

3. ماذا طَلَبَ الجِنِّيُّ مِنَ التّاجِرِ أَنْ يَفْعَلَ لِيُسامِحَهُ؟

4. مَنْ هُوَ الشَّخْصُ الَّذي وَجَدَهُ التّاجِرُ لِيُساعِدَهُ؟

5. كَيْفَ أَقْنَعَ الرَّجُلُ العَجوزُ الجِنِّيَّ بِعَدَمِ قَتْلِ التّاجِرِ؟

Answers

1. بَدَأَتْ شَهْرَزادُ تَرْوي قِصَّةَ التّاجِرِ وَالجِنِّيِّ العَجيبِ.

2. غَضِبَ الجِنِّيُّ لِأَنَّ التّاجِرَ دَمَّرَ بَيْتَهُ.

3. طَلَبَ الجِنِّيُّ مِنَ التّاجِرِ أَنْ يَأْتِيَ بِشَخْصٍ يُقْنِعُ الجِنِّيَّ بِأَلّا يَقْتُلَهُ.

4. وَجَدَ التّاجِرُ رَجُلًا عَجوزًا حَكيمًا كانَ يَعْرِفُ الكَثيرَ عَنِ الجِنِّ وَعالَمِهِمْ.

5. أَقْنَعَ الرَّجُلُ العَجوزُ الجِنِّيَّ بِعَدَمِ قَتْلِ التّاجِرِ عَنْ طَريقِ سَرْدِ قِصَّةٍ مُثيرَةٍ عَنِ المُغامَرَةِ وَالشَّجاعَةِ وَالتَّضْحِيَةِ، وَبَعْدَ سَماعِ الجِنِّيِّ لِلْقِصَّةِ، وافَقَ عَلى سَماحِهِ لِلتّاجِرِ بِالْعَيْشِ بِشَرْطِ أَنْ يَحْذَرَ مِنْ تَكْرارِ مِثْلِ هَذا الخَطَأِ مُسْتَقْبَلًا.

Chapter 2: The Genie and the Merchant

On the following night, King Shahryar asked Scheherazade to tell him a new story. Scheherazade began to narrate the tale of the merchant and the marvelous genie.

One day, a wealthy merchant went on a long journey to sell his goods. After a tiring journey, he stopped to rest under a tree. While he was sitting there, a giant and angry genie appeared.

The genie said to the merchant, "I will kill you because you destroyed my home." The merchant was frightened and did not understand what the genie meant. He asked the genie to explain the reason for his anger.

When you came and removed this wooden log to sit on it, some things fell on me and destroyed my small home where I lived.

The merchant was saddened by what had happened, but he did not know that there was a genie's home behind the tree. He asked the genie to show mercy and forgive him.

The genie said, "I will give you a chance to bring someone who can convince me not to kill you. If you fail, I will kill you for sure."

The merchant went on a long journey in search of someone to help him. Finally, he found a wise old man who knew a lot about genies and their world.

The old man listened to the merchant's story and decided to help him. They went together to the place of the tree where the genie was waiting for them.

The old man said to the genie, "I want to tell you a story before you decide the fate of this merchant. If you like the story, I hope you will forgive him and let him live."

The genie agreed to hear the story. The old man began to narrate an exciting tale of adventure, bravery, and sacrifice. The story was full of suspense and important lessons.

After hearing the story, the genie said, "I really liked the story and learned great lessons from it. I will forgive the merchant on the condition that he would be careful not to repeat such a mistake in the future."

The merchant thanked the genie for his mercy and promised to be more careful and compassionate in his actions. He also thanked the old man for his help and wisdom. Then, the merchant returned to his village and family and pledged to be more cautious and compassionate in his dealings with nature and its creatures.

On the following night, Scheherazade finished narrating the tale of the merchant and the genie. King Shahryar was impressed by this story and wanted to hear more wonderful stories told by Scheherazade. Thus, Scheherazade continued to narrate her stories to the king night after night, teaching him and his people important lessons about life, wisdom, and justice.

Questions
1. What is the story Scheherazade began to tell on the second night?
2. Why was the genie angry with the merchant?
3. What did the genie ask the merchant to do to forgive him?
4. Who did the merchant find to help him?
5. How did the old man convince the genie not to kill the merchant?

Answers
1. Scheherazade began to tell the story of the merchant and the strange genie.
2. The genie was angry because the merchant destroyed his home.
3. The genie asked the merchant to bring someone who could convince the genie not to kill him.
4. The merchant found a wise old man who knew a lot about genie and their world to help him.
5. The old man convinced the genie not to kill the merchant by telling an exciting story of adventure, bravery, and sacrifice. After hearing the story, the genie agreed to spare the merchant's life on the condition that he would be careful not to repeat such a mistake in the future.

الفَصْلُ الثَّالِثُ
الصَّيَّادُ وَالسَّمَكَةُ الذَّهَبِيَّةُ

في اللَّيْلَةِ التَّالِيَةِ، بَدَأَتْ شَهْرَزادُ تَرْوي قِصَّةَ السَّمَكَةِ الذَّهَبِيَّةِ وَالصَّيَّادِ لِلْمَلِكِ شَهْرَيارَ.

كانَ هُناكَ صَيَّادٌ فَقيرٌ يَعيشُ في قَرْيَةٍ ساحِلِيَّةٍ بَسيطَةٍ مَعَ زَوْجَتِهِ. كانَ يَصْطادُ الأَسْماكَ يَوْمِيًّا لِكَيْ يُعيلَ أُسْرَتَهُ. ذاتَ يَوْمٍ، اِصْطادَ

سَمَكَةٌ ذَهَبِيَّةٌ جَمِيلَةٌ كَانَتْ تَتَأَلَّقُ بِالبَرِيقِ وَالجَمَالِ. تَحَدَّثَتِ السَّمَكَةُ إِلَيْهِ قَائِلَةً: "أَنَا سَمَكَةٌ سِحْرِيَّةٌ، وَإِذَا أَطْلَقْتَنِي سَأُحَقِّقُ لَكَ ثَلَاثَ أُمْنِيَّاتٍ تُرِيدُهَا."

فَكَّرَ الصَّيَّادُ فِي الأُمُورِ الَّتِي يَحْتَاجُهَا وَقَرَّرَ أَنْ يَطْلُبَ مِنَ السَّمَكَةِ الذَّهَبِيَّةِ أَنْ تَمْنَحَهُ الثَّرْوَةَ وَالسَّعَادَةَ وَالصِّحَّةَ الجَيِّدَةَ. أَطْلَقَ السَّمَكَةَ الذَّهَبِيَّةَ وَتَحَقَّقَتْ أُمْنِيَّاتُهُ.

تَحَسَّنَتْ حَيَاةُ الصَّيَّادِ وَزَوْجَتِهِ كَثِيرًا بِفَضْلِ الأُمْنِيَّاتِ الَّتِي حَقَّقَتْهَا لَهُمُ السَّمَكَةُ الذَّهَبِيَّةُ. لَكِنْ مَعَ مُرُورِ الوَقْتِ، بَدَأَتْ زَوْجَتُهُ تَطْمَعُ فِي المَزِيدِ وَطَلَبَتْ مِنْ زَوْجِهَا أَنْ يَعُودَ إِلَى السَّمَكَةِ الذَّهَبِيَّةِ لِيَطْلُبَ المَزِيدَ مِنِ الأُمْنِيَّاتِ.

عَادَ الصَّيَّادُ إِلَى الشَّاطِئِ حَيْثُ اصْطَادَ السَّمَكَةَ الذَّهَبِيَّةَ، وَنَادَاهَا. ظَهَرَتِ السَّمَكَةُ الذَّهَبِيَّةُ مَرَّةً أُخْرَى وَاسْتَمَعَتْ إِلَى طَلَبَاتِ الصَّيَّادِ. لَكِنْ هَذِهِ المَرَّةَ، حَذَّرَتْهُ السَّمَكَةُ الذَّهَبِيَّةُ مِنْ أَنَّ الطَّمَعَ لَنْ يَجْلِبَ لَهُمُ السَّعَادَةَ وَالرَّاحَةَ.

تَعَلَّمَ الصَّيَّادُ وَزَوْجَتُهُ الدَّرْسَ القَيِّمَ الَّذي أرادَتِ السَّمَكَةُ الذَّهَبِيَّةُ أَنْ تُعَلِّمَهُما إِيَّاهُ، وَقَرَّرا أَنْ يَكْتَفِيا بِما لَدَيْهِما، وَأَنْ يَعيشا حَياةً بَسيطَةً وَسَعيدَةً بِدونِ طَمَعٍ.

اِنْتَهَتْ شَهْرَزادُ مِنْ سَرْدِ قِصَّةِ السَّمَكَةِ الذَّهَبِيَّةِ وَالصَّيَّادِ. كانَ المَلِكُ شَهْرَيارُ مُعْجَبًا بِهَذِهِ القِصَّةِ وَأَرادَ سَماعَ المَزيدِ مِنَ القِصَصِ الَّتي تَحْمِلُ دُروسًا قَيِّمَةً وَعِبَرًا هامَّةً. وَبِهَذِهِ الطَّريقَةِ، اِسْتَمَرَّتْ شَهْرَزادُ في سَرْدِ قِصَصِها لِلْمَلِكِ شَهْرَيارَ لَيْلَةً بَعْدَ لَيْلَةٍ، مُعَلِّمَةً إِيَّاهُ وَشَعْبَهُ دُروسًا هامَّةً عَنِ الرِّضا وَالتَّواضُعِ وَالسَّعادَةِ.

Questions

١. ما هِيَ القِصَّةُ الَّتي بَدَأَتْ شَهْرَزادُ تَرويها في اللَّيْلَةِ السَّابِعَةِ؟

٢. ماذا اصْطادَ الصَّيّادُ في يَوْمِ حَظِّهِ؟

٣. ماذا قالَتِ السَّمَكَةُ الذَّهَبِيَّةُ لِلصَّيّادِ؟

٤. ما هِيَ الأُمْنِيّاتُ الَّتي طَلَبَها الصَّيّادُ مِنَ السَّمَكَةِ الذَّهَبِيَّةِ؟

٥. كَيْفَ تَعَلَّمَ الصَّيّادُ وَزَوْجَتُهُ الدَّرْسَ القَيِّمَ الَّذي أَرادَتِ السَّمَكَةُ الذَّهَبِيَّةُ أَنْ تُعَلِّمَهُما إِيّاهُ؟

Answers

1. بَدَأَتْ شَهْرَزادُ تَرْوي قِصَّةَ السَّمَكَةِ الذَّهَبِيَّةِ وَالصَّيّادِ.

2. اِصْطادُ الصَّيّادُ سَمَكَةً ذَهَبِيَّةً جَميلَةً كانَتْ تَتَأَلَّقُ بِالْبَريقِ وَالجَمالِ.

3. قالَتِ السَّمَكَةُ الذَّهَبِيَّةُ لِلصَّيّادِ إِنَّها سَمَكَةٌ سِحْرِيَّةٌ، وَإِنَّهُ إِذا أَطْلَقَها سَتُحَقِّقُ لَهُ ثَلاثَ أُمْنِيّاتٍ يُريدُها.

4. طَلَبَ الصَّيّادُ مِنَ السَّمَكَةِ الذَّهَبِيَّةِ أَنْ تَمْنَحَهُ الثَّرْوَةَ وَالسَّعادَةَ وَالصِّحَّةَ الجَيِّدَةَ.

5. حَذَّرَتِ السَّمَكَةُ الذَّهَبِيَّةُ الصَّيّادَ وَزَوْجَتَهُ مِنْ أَنَّ الطَّمَعَ لَنْ يَجْلِبَ لَهُما السَّعادَةَ وَالرّاحَةَ. تَعَلَّمَ الصَّيّادُ وَزَوْجَتُهُ الدَّرْسَ القَيِّمَ وَقَرَّرا أَنْ يَكْتَفِيا بِما لَدَيْهِما وَأَنْ يَعيشا حَياةً بَسيطَةً وَسَعيدَةً بِدونِ طَمَعٍ.

Chapter 3: The Fisherman and the Golden Fish

On the following night, Scheherazade began to tell the story of the Golden Fish and the Fisherman to King Shahryar.

There was a poor fisherman who lived in a simple coastal village with his wife. He fished every day to provide for his family. One day, he caught a beautiful golden fish that shimmered with brilliance and beauty. The fish spoke to him, saying, "I am a magical fish, and if you release me, I will grant you three wishes."

The fisherman thought about what he needed and decided to ask the golden fish to grant him wealth, happiness, and good health. He released the golden fish, and his wishes came true. The life of the fisherman and his wife improved greatly thanks to the wishes granted by the golden fish. But over time, his wife became greedy and asked her husband to return to the golden fish to ask for more wishes.

The fisherman returned to the beach, where he caught the golden fish and called out to it. The golden fish appeared again and listened to the fisherman's requests. But this time, the golden fish warned him that greed would not bring them happiness and peace.

The fisherman and his wife learned the valuable lesson that the golden fish wanted to teach them, and they decided to be content with what they had and live a simple and happy life without greed.

Scheherazade finished telling the story of the Golden Fish and the Fisherman. King Shahryar was impressed by this story and wanted to hear more stories that carry valuable lessons and important morals. In this way, Scheherazade continued to tell her stories to King Shahryar night after night, teaching him and his people important lessons about contentment, humility, and happiness.

Questions
1. What story did Scheherazade begin telling on the seventh night?
2. What did the fisherman catch on his lucky day?
3. What did the golden fish say to the fisherman?
4. What wishes did the fisherman ask the golden fish to grant him?
5. How did the fisherman and his wife learn the valuable lesson that the golden fish wanted to teach them?

Answers
1. Scheherazade began telling the story of the golden fish and the fisherman.
2. The fisherman caught a beautiful golden fish that sparkled with radiance and beauty.
3. The golden fish told the fisherman that it was a magical fish, and if he released it, it would grant him three wishes that he desired.

4. The fisherman asked the golden fish to grant him wealth, happiness, and good health.
5. The golden fish warned the fisherman and his wife that greed would not bring them happiness and peace. The fisherman and his wife learned a valuable lesson and decided to be content with what they had and live a simple and happy life without greed.

الفَصْلُ الرَّابِعُ
عَلاءُ الدّينِ وَالمِصْباحُ السِّحْرِيُّ

في اللَّيْلَةِ التّالِيَةِ، بَدَأَتْ شَهْرَزادُ تَرْوي قِصَّةَ عَلاءِ الدّينِ وَالمِصْباحِ السِّحْرِيِّ لِلْمَلِكِ شَهْرَيارَ.

كانَ عَلاءُ الدّينِ فَتًى فَقيرًا يَعيشُ في مَدينَةٍ صَغيرَةٍ مَعَ والِدَتِهِ. ذاتَ يَوْمٍ، التَقى بِرَجُلٍ غَريبٍ قالَ إِنَّهُ عَمُّهُ وَعَرَضَ عَلَيْهِ مُغامَرَةً

لِلْبَحْثِ عَنْ كَنْزٍ مَدْفونٍ. بِالرَّغْمِ مِنْ شُكوكِ عَلاءِ الدّينِ، قَرَّرَ الِانْضِمامَ إِلى الرَّجُلِ الغَريبِ في رِحْلَتِهِ.

وَصَلا إِلى مَغارَةٍ مُظْلِمَةٍ حَيْثُ كانَ الكَنْزُ مَخْفِيًّا. طَلَبَ الرَّجُلُ الغَريبُ مِنْ عَلاءِ الدّينِ أَنْ يَدْخُلَ المَغارَةَ وَيَأْخُذَ مِصْباحًا قَديمًا كانَ مَوْجودًا هُناكَ. لَكِنْ بِمُجَرَّدِ حُصولِ عَلاءِ الدّينِ عَلى المِصْباحِ، أَغْلَقَ الرَّجُلُ الغَريبُ المَغارَةَ وَتَرَكَهُ مُحْتَجَزًا بِداخِلِها.

في مُحاوَلَةٍ لِلْخُروجِ مِنَ المَغارَةِ، بَدَأَ عَلاءُ الدّينِ يَبْحَثُ عَنْ طَريقٍ لِلْخُروجِ. وَجَدَ المِصْباحَ القَديمَ وَرَأى أَنَّهُ قَدْ يَكونُ مُفيدًا لِإِضاءَةِ المَغارَةِ المُظْلِمَةِ وَالبَحْثِ عَنِ المَخْرَجِ. بَدَأَ عَلاءُ الدّينِ بِمَسْحِ الغُبارِ عَنِ المِصْباحِ، وَفَجْأَةً ظَهَرَ جِنِّيٌّ عِمْلاقٌ. قالَ الجِنِّيُّ: "أَنا جِنِّيُّ المِصْباحِ السِّحْرِيِّ، وَأَنا هُنا لِتَحْقيقِ ثَلاثِ أُمْنِيّاتٍ تَطْلُبُها."

بِمُساعَدَةِ الجِنِّيِّ، تَمَكَّنَ عَلاءُ الدِّينِ مِنَ الهُروبِ مِنَ المَغارَةِ وَعادَ إِلى المَدينَةِ. طَلَبَ مِنَ الجِنِّيِّ تَحْقيقَ أُمْنِيّاتِهِ: أَنْ يُصْبِحَ غَنِيًّا، أَنْ يَتَزَوَّجَ الأَميرَةَ وَأَنْ يُصْبِحَ سُلْطانَ المَدينَةِ.

تَحَقَّقَتْ جَميعُ أُمْنِيّاتِ عَلاءِ الدِّينِ، وَأَصْبَحَ غَنِيًّا، وَتَزَوَّجَ الأَميرَةَ، وَتَوَلّى حُكْمَ المَدينَةِ كَسُلْطانٍ. لَكِنَّ الرَّجُلَ الغَريبَ الَّذي كانَ يَدَّعي أَنَّهُ عَمُّهُ كانَ يُخَطِّطُ لِسَرِقَةِ المِصْباحِ السِّحْرِيِّ وَاسْتِخْدامِ قُوَّتِهِ لِلسَّيْطَرَةِ عَلى المَدينَةِ.

في يَوْمٍ مِنَ الأَيّامِ، تَمَكَّنَ الرَّجُلُ الغَريبُ مِنْ سَرِقَةِ المِصْباحِ، وَطَلَبَ مِنَ الجِنِّيِّ أَنْ يَنْقُلَ القَصْرَ الَّذي كانَ يَعيشُ فيهِ عَلاءُ الدِّينِ وَالأَميرَةُ إِلى بِلادٍ بَعيدَةٍ. شَعَرَ عَلاءُ الدِّينِ بِاليَأْسِ، لَكِنَّهُ تَذَكَّرَ خاتَمًا سِحْرِيًّا كانَ قَدْ أَعْطاهُ لَهُ الرَّجُلُ الغَريبُ قَبْلَ دُخولِهِ المَغارَةَ.

اِسْتَخْدَمَ عَلاءُ الدِّينِ الخاتَمَ السِّحْرِيَّ لِاسْتِدْعاءِ جِنِّيٍّ آخَرَ كانَ يَخْدِمُهُ. طَلَبَ مِنَ الجِنِّيِّ أَنْ يَنْقُلَهُ إِلى القَصْرِ وَيُعيدَهُ إِلى المَدينَةِ. بِمُساعَدَةِ الجِنِّيِّ وَالأَميرَةِ، تَمَكَّنَ عَلاءُ الدِّينِ مِنَ اسْتِعادَةِ المِصْباحِ السِّحْرِيِّ وَهَزيمَةِ الرَّجُلِ الغَريبِ.

عادَ عَلاءُ الدّينِ إلى حَياتِهِ كَسُلْطانٍ وَعاشَ سَعيدًا مَعَ الأَميرَةِ. تَعَلَّمَ عَلاءُ الدّينِ العَديدَ مِنَ الدُّروسِ عَنِ الثِّقَةِ والشَّجاعَةِ والحُبِّ.

اِنْتَهَتْ شَهْرَزادُ مِنْ سَرْدِ قِصَّةِ عَلاءِ الدّينِ والمِصْباحِ السِّحْرِيِّ. كانَ المَلِكُ شَهْرَيارُ مُعْجَبًا بِهَذِهِ القِصَّةِ، وَأَرادَ سَماعَ المَزيدِ مِنَ القِصَصِ المُلْهِمَةِ والمُثيرَةِ. وَهَكَذا، اِسْتَمَرَّتْ شَهْرَزادُ في سَرْدِ قِصَصِها لِلْمَلِكِ شَهْرَيارَ لَيْلَةً بَعْدَ لَيْلَةٍ، مُعَلِّمَةً إِيّاهُ وَشَعْبَهُ دُروسًا هامَّةً عَنِ الحَياةِ والحِكْمَةِ والعَدْلِ.

Questions

1. ما هِيَ القِصَّةُ الَّتي بَدَأَتْ شَهْرَزادُ تَرويها في اللَّيْلَةِ الرّابِعَةِ؟

2. ماذا عَرَضَ الرَّجُلُ الغَريبُ عَلى عَلاءِ الدّينِ؟

3. ماذا وَجَدَ عَلاءُ الدّينِ داخِلَ المَغارَةِ؟

4. ماذا فَعَلَ الجِنِّيُّ الَّذي خَرَجَ مِنَ المِصْباحِ السِّحْرِيِّ؟

5. ما الدُّروسُ الَّتي تَعَلَّمَها عَلاءُ الدّينِ مِنْ هَذِهِ القِصَّةِ؟

Answers

١. بَدَأَتْ شَهْرَزادُ تَرْوي قِصَّةَ عَلاءِ الدّينِ وَالمِصْباحِ السِّحْرِيِّ.

٢. عَرَضَ الرَّجُلُ الغَريبُ عَلى عَلاءِ الدّينِ مُغامَرَةً لِلْبَحْثِ عَنْ كَنْزٍ مَدْفونٍ.

٣. وَجَدَ عَلاءُ الدّينِ مِصْباحًا قَديمًا داخِلَ المَغارَةِ.

٤. قالَ الجِنِّيُّ إِنَّهُ هُنا لِتَحْقيقِ ثَلاثِ أُمْنِيّاتٍ يَطْلُبُها عَلاءُ الدّينِ.

٥. تَعَلَّمَ عَلاءُ الدّينِ العَديدَ مِنَ الدُّروسِ عَنِ الثِّقَةِ وَالشَّجاعَةِ وَالحُبِّ.

Chapter 4: Aladdin and the Magic Lamp

On the next night, Scheherazade began to tell the story of Aladdin and the Magic Lamp to King Shahryar.

Aladdin was a poor boy who lived in a small city with his mother. One day, he met a strange man who claimed to be his uncle and offered him an adventure to search for a buried treasure. Despite Aladdin's suspicions, he decided to join the stranger on his journey.

They arrived at a dark cave where the treasure was hidden. The strange man asked Aladdin to enter the cave and take an old lamp that was there. But as soon as Aladdin got the lamp, the strange man closed the cave, trapping him inside.

In an attempt to get out of the cave, Aladdin started looking for a way out. He found the old lamp and thought it might be useful to light up the dark cave and to search for the exit. Aladdin started to wipe the dust off the lamp, and suddenly a giant genie appeared. The genie said, "I am the genie of the magic lamp, and I am here to grant three wishes that you make."

With the genie's help, Aladdin was able to escape from the cave and return to the city. He asked the genie to grant his wishes: to become rich, to marry the princess, and to become the sultan of the city.

All of Aladdin's wishes came true, and he became rich, married the princess, and became the sultan of the city. But the strange man who claimed to be his uncle was planning to steal the magic lamp and use its power to control the city.

One day, the strange man was able to steal the lamp and asked the genie to transport the palace where Aladdin and the princess lived to a distant land. Aladdin felt hopeless, but he remembered a magical ring that the strange man had given him before entering the cave.

Aladdin used the magical ring to summon another genie who served him. He asked the genie to transport him to the palace and return him to the city. With the help of the genie and the princess, Aladdin was able to retrieve the magic lamp and defeat the strange man.

Aladdin returned to his life as a sultan and lived happily with the princess. He learned many lessons about trust, courage, and love.

Scheherazade finished telling the story of Aladdin and the Magic Lamp. King Shahryar was impressed by this story and wanted to hear more inspiring and exciting stories. And so, Scheherazade continued to tell her stories to King Shahryar night after night, teaching him and his people important lessons about life, wisdom, and justice.

Questions
1. What story did Scheherazade begin telling on the fourth night?
2. What did the strange man offer Aladdin?
3. What did Aladdin find inside the cave?
4. What did the genie that came out of the magic lamp do?
5. What lessons did Aladdin learn from this story?

Answers
1. Scheherazade began telling the story of Aladdin and the Magic Lamp to King Shahryar.
2. The strange man offered Aladdin an adventure to search for a buried treasure.
3. Aladdin found an old lamp inside the cave.
4. The genie said he was there to grant three wishes that Aladdin requested.
5. Aladdin learned many lessons about trust, courage, and love.

الفَصْلُ الخامِسُ
عَلي بابا وَالأَرْبَعون لِصًّا

في اللَّيْلَةِ التّالِيَةِ، بَدَأَتْ شَهْرَزاد تَرْوي قِصَّةَ عَلي بابا وَالأَرْبَعينَ لِصًّا لِلْمَلِكِ شَهْرَيارَ.

كانَ عَلي بابا رَجُلًا بَسيطًا يَعيشُ في قَرْيَةٍ صَغيرَةٍ وَيَعْمَلُ كَحَطّابٍ. ذاتَ يَوْمٍ، وَبَيْنَما كانَ يَحْتَطِبُ في الغابَةِ، رَأى مَجْموعَةً مِنَ

اللُّصوصِ يَدْخُلونَ مَغارَةً مَخْفِيَّةً. قالَ قائِدُ اللُّصوصِ كَلِمَةً سِرِّيَّةً: "اِفْتَحْ يا سِمْسِمْ"، فُتِحَتِ البَوّابَةُ الصَّخْرِيَّةُ وَدَخَلَ اللُّصوصُ.

بَعْدَ أَنْ غادَرَ اللُّصوصُ المَغارَةَ، ذَهَبَ عَلي بابا وَقالَ الكَلِمَةَ السِّرِّيَّةَ لِيَدْخُلَ المَغارَةَ. وَجَدَ الكَنْزَ الَّذي جَمَعَهُ اللُّصوصُ وَقَرَّرَ أَنْ يَأْخُذَ جُزْءًا مِنْهُ لِيُساعِدَ عائِلَتَهُ وَجيرانَهُ.

عَلِمَتْ مَرْجانَةُ، الخادِمَةُ المُخْلِصَةُ لِعَلي بابا، بِسِرِّ الكَنْزِ وَمَغارَةِ اللُّصوصِ. عِنْدَما عَلِمَ قائِدُ اللُّصوصِ بِأَنَّ عَلي بابا قَدِ اكْتَشَفَ سِرَّهُمْ، قَرَّرَ الاِنْتِقامَ مِنْهُ وَاسْتِعادَةَ الكَنْزِ المَسْروقِ.

تَصَدَّتْ مَرْجانَةُ لِمُحاوَلاتِ اللُّصوصِ لِقَتْلِ عَلي بابا وَأُسْرَتِهِ، حَتّى تَمَكَّنَتْ في النِّهايَةِ مِنْ قَتْلِ قائِدِ اللُّصوصِ وَإِنْقاذِ عَلي بابا. اِسْتَخْدَمَ عَلي بابا جُزْءًا مِنَ الكَنْزِ لِيَعيشَ حَياةً أَفْضَلَ مَعَ عائِلَتِهِ وَيُساعِدَ الفُقَراءَ وَالمُحْتاجينَ في القَرْيَةِ.

اِنْتَهَتْ شَهْرَزادُ مِنْ سَرْدِ قِصَّةِ عَلي بابا وَالأَرْبَعينَ لِصًّا. كانَ المَلِكُ شَهْرَيارُ مُنْبَهِرًا بِالْقِصَّةِ وَأَرادَ سَماعَ المَزيدِ مِنَ القِصَصِ الَّتي تَحْمِلُ دُروسًا قَيِّمَةً وَعِبَرًا هامَّةً. وَبِهَذا الشَّكْلِ، اِسْتَمَرَّتْ شَهْرَزادُ في سَرْدِ قِصَصِها لِلْمَلِكِ شَهْرَيارَ لَيْلَةً بَعْدَ لَيْلَةٍ، مُعَلِّمَةً إيَّاهُ وَشَعْبَهُ دُروسًا هامَّةً عَنِ الحَياةِ وَالشَّجاعَةِ وَالصَّداقَةِ.

Questions

1. ما هِيَ القِصَّةُ الَّتي بَدَأَتْ شَهْرَزادُ تَرْويها في اللَّيْلَةِ الخامِسَةِ؟

2. ما هِيَ المِهْنَةُ الَّتي كانَ يَعْمَلُ بِها عَلي بابا؟

3. ما الكَلِمَةُ السِّرِّيَّةُ الَّتي اسْتَخْدَمَها قائِدُ اللُّصوصِ لِفَتْحِ بَوّابَةِ المَغارَةِ؟

4. مَنْ هِيَ مَرْجانَةُ وَما دَوْرُها في القِصَّةِ؟

5. ماذا فَعَلَ عَلي بابًا بِالْكَنْزِ الَّذي وَجَدَهُ في المَغارَةِ؟

Answers

1. بَدَأَتْ شَهْرَزادُ تَروي قِصَّةَ عَلي بابا وَالْأَرْبَعينَ لِصًّا.

2. كانَ عَلي بابا يَعْمَلُ حَطَّابًا.

3. الْكَلِمَةُ السِّرِّيَّةُ الَّتي اسْتَخْدَمَها قائِدُ اللُّصوصِ كانَتْ "اِفْتَحْ يا سِمْسِمْ".

4. مَرْجانَةُ هِيَ الْخادِمَةُ الْمُخْلِصَةُ لِعَلي بابا، عَلِمَتْ بِسِرِّ الْكَنْزِ وَمَغارَةِ اللُّصوصِ، وَتَصَدَّتْ لِمُحاوَلاتِ اللُّصوصِ لِقَتْلِ عَلي بابا وَأُسْرَتِهِ، وَفي النِّهايَةِ تَمَكَّنَتْ مِنْ قَتْلِ قائِدِ اللُّصوصِ وَإِنْقاذِ عَلي بابا.

5. اِسْتَخْدَمَ عَلي بابا جُزْءًا مِنَ الْكَنْزِ لِيَعيشَ حَياةً أَفْضَلَ مَعَ عائِلَتِهِ وَيُساعِدَ الْفُقَراءَ وَالْمُحْتاجينَ في الْقَرْيَةِ.

Chapter 5: Ali Baba and the Forty Thieves

On the next night, Scheherazade began to tell the story of Ali Baba and the Forty Thieves to King Shahryar.
Ali Baba was a simple man who lived in a small village and worked as a woodcutter. One day while he was working in the forest, he saw a group of thieves entering a hidden cave. The leader of the thieves said a secret word, "Open Sesame," and the rock gate opened for them to enter.
After the thieves left the cave, Ali Baba went to the cave and said the secret word, entering the cave. He found the treasure that the thieves had collected and decided to take part of it to help his family and neighbors.
Morgiana, Ali Baba's loyal servant, learned about the treasure and the cave of the thieves. When the leader of the thieves learned that Ali Baba had discovered their secret, he decided to take revenge on him and get back the stolen treasure.
Morgiana fought against the attempts of the thieves to kill Ali Baba and his family until she finally managed to kill the leader of the thieves and save Ali Baba. Ali Baba used a part of the treasure to live a better life with his family and help the poor and needy in the village.
Scheherazade finished telling the story of Ali Baba and the Forty Thieves. King Shahryar was amazed by the story and wanted to hear more stories that carry valuable lessons and important messages. And so, Scheherazade continued to tell her stories to King Shahryar night after night, teaching him

and his people important lessons about life, courage, and friendship.

Questions
1. What is the story that Scheherazade began to tell on the fifth night?
2. What was Ali Baba's profession?
3. What was the secret word used by the leader of the thieves to open the cave gate?
4. Who is Morgiana, and what was her role in the story?
5. What did Ali Baba do with the treasure he found in the cave?

Answers
1. Scheherazade began to tell the story of Ali Baba and the Forty Thieves.
2. Ali Baba worked as a woodcutter.
3. The secret word used by the leader of the thieves was "Open Sesame."
4. Morgiana was Ali Baba's loyal servant. She discovered the secret of the treasure and the thieves' cave, and she foiled the attempts of the thieves to kill Ali Baba and his family. In the end, she managed to kill the leader of the thieves and save Ali Baba.
5. Ali Baba used part of the treasure to live a better life with his family and help the poor and needy in the village.

الفَصْلُ السَّادِسُ
الفَلَّاحُ الذَّكِيُّ وَالجِنِّيُّ المُشَاغِبُ

في اللَّيْلَةِ السَّادِسَةِ، بَدَأَتْ شَهْرَزادُ تَرْوي قِصَّةَ الفَلَّاحِ الذَّكِيِّ وَالجِنِّيِّ المُشاغِبِ لِلْمَلِكِ شَهْرَيارَ.

كانَ هُناكَ فَلَّاحٌ فَقيرٌ يَعْمَلُ بِجِدٍّ لِكَسْبِ قوتِ أُسْرَتِهِ. في يَوْمٍ مِنَ الأَيَّامِ، وَجَدَ الفَلَّاحُ إِناءً نُحاسِيًّا قَديمًا مَدْفونًا في حَقْلِهِ. قَرَّرَ الفَلَّاحُ

فَتْحَ الإِناءِ لِيَجِدَ ما بِداخِلِهِ.

بِمُجَرَّدِ فَتْحِ الإِناءِ، انْبَعَثَ مِنْهُ جِنِّيٌّ عِمْلاقٌ يُريدُ الاِنْتِقامَ مِنَ الفَلّاحِ لِأَنَّهُ أَقْلَقَ نَوْمَتَهُ الهانِئَةَ الطَّويلَةَ. كانَ الجِنِّيُّ يَعْتَقِدُ أَنَّ الفَلّاحَ سَيَطْلُبُ مِنْهُ أُمْنِيَّةً لِتَحْسينِ حَياتِهِ، لَكِنَّ الفَلّاحَ كانَ ذَكِيًّا وَوَضَعَ خُطَّةً لِلتَّعامُلِ مَعَ الجِنِّيِّ.

قالَ الفَلّاحُ لِلجِنِّيِّ إِنَّهُ لا يُصَدِّقُ قُوَّتَهُ وَلا يَعْتَقِدُ أَنَّهُ سَيَتَمَكَّنُ مِنَ العَوْدَةِ إِلى الإِناءِ. شَعَرَ الجِنِّيُّ بِالغَضَبِ وَالإِهانَةِ، فَقَرَّرَ إِثْباتَ قُوَّتِهِ لِلفَلّاحِ وَعادَ إِلى الإِناءِ فَوْرًا. بِمُجَرَّدِ عَوْدَةِ الجِنِّيِّ إِلى الإِناءِ، أَغْلَقَ الفَلّاحُ الغِطاءَ بِسُرورٍ.

وَعَدَ الفَلّاحُ الجِنِّيَّ أَنَّهُ سَيُطْلِقُ سَراحَهُ مَرَّةً أُخْرى إِذا وَعَدَ بِعَدَمِ إيذاءِ أَيِّ شَخْصٍ وَمُساعَدَةِ الفَلّاحِ وَأُسْرَتِهِ. وافَقَ الجِنِّيُّ عَلى الشُّروطِ وَتَعاوَنَ مَعَ الفَلّاحِ، وَتَحَسَّنَتْ حَياةُ الفَلّاحِ وَأُسْرَتِهِ بِفَضْلِ قُوَّةِ الجِنِّيِّ وَذَكاءِ الفَلّاحِ.

اِنْتَهَتْ شَهْرَزادُ مِنْ سَرْدِ قِصَّةِ الفَلّاحِ الذَّكِيِّ وَالجِنِّيِّ المُشاغِبِ. كانَ المَلِكُ شَهْرَيارُ مُعْجَبًا بِهَذِهِ القِصَّةِ وَأرادَ سَماعَ المَزيدِ مِنَ القِصَصِ الَّتي تَحْمِلُ دُروسًا قَيِّمَةً وَعِبَرًا هامَّةً عَنِ الذَّكاءِ وَالمَكْرِ وَالتَّعاوُنِ بَيْنَ البَشَرِ وَالجِنِّ.

Questions

1. ما هِيَ القِصَّةُ الَّتي بَدَأَتْ شَهْرَزادُ تَرْويها في اللَّيْلَةِ السّادِسَةِ؟

2. ماذا وَجَدَ الفَلّاحُ في حَقْلِهِ؟

3. ماذا كانَ الجِنِّيُّ يَظُنُّ عِنْدَما أَطْلَقَ الفَلاحُ سَراحَهُ؟

4. ما هِيَ الخُطَّةُ الَّتي وَضَعَها الفَلّاحُ لِلتَّعامُلِ مَعَ الجِنِّيِّ؟

5. كَيْفَ تَحَسَّنَتْ حَياةُ الفَلّاحِ وَأُسْرَتِهِ؟

Answers

1. بَدَأَتْ شَهْرَزادُ تَرْوي قِصَّةَ الفَلّاحِ الذَّكِيِّ وَالجِنِّيِّ المُشاغِبِ.

2. وَجَدَ الفَلّاحُ إناءَ نُحاسِيًّا قَديمًا مَدْفونًا في حَقْلِهِ.

3. كانَ الجِنِّيُّ يَعْتَقِدُ أَنَّ الفَلّاحَ سَيَطْلُبُ مِنْهُ أُمْنِيَةً لِتَحْسينِ حَياتِهِ.

4. قالَ الفَلّاحُ لِلْجِنِّيِّ إِنَّهُ لا يُصَدِّقُ قُوَّتَهُ وَلا يَعْتَقِدُ أَنَّهُ سَيَتَمَكَّنُ مِنَ العَوْدَةِ إِلى الإِناءِ. شَعَرَ الجِنِّيُّ بِالْغَضَبِ وَالإِهانَةِ، فَقَرَّرَ إِثْباتَ قُوَّتِهِ لِلْفَلّاحِ وَعادَ إِلى الإِناءِ فَوْرًا. بِمُجَرَّدِ عَوْدَةِ الجِنِّيِّ إِلى الإِناءِ، أَغْلَقَ الفَلّاحُ الغِطاءَ بِسُرورٍ.

5. تَحَسَّنَتْ حَياةُ الفَلّاحِ وَأُسْرَتِهِ بِفَضْلِ قُوَّةِ الجِنِّيِّ وَذَكاءِ الفَلّاحِ، بَعْدَ أَنْ وَعَدَ الجِنِّيُّ بِعَدَمِ إيذاءِ أَيِّ شَخْصٍ، وَمُساعَدَةِ الفَلّاحِ وَأُسْرَتِهِ.

Chapter 6: The Clever Farmer and the Mischievous Genie

On the sixth night, Scheherazade began to tell the story of the Clever Farmer and the Mischievous Genie to King Shahryar.

There was a poor farmer who worked hard to provide for his family. One day, he found an old copper vessel buried in his field. The farmer decided to open the vessel to see what was inside.

As soon as he opened the vessel, a giant genie emerged from it, seeking revenge on the farmer for interrupting his long slumber. The genie thought the farmer would ask for a wish to improve his life, but the farmer was clever and had a plan to deal with the genie.

The farmer told the genie that he did not believe in his power and did not think he could return to the vessel. The genie felt angry and humiliated, so he decided to prove his power to the farmer and immediately returned to the vessel. Once the genie was back in the vessel, the farmer closed the lid with joy.

The farmer promised to release the genie again if he promised not to harm anyone and to help the farmer and his family. The genie agreed to the conditions and cooperated with the farmer, and the life of the farmer and his family improved thanks to the genie's power and the farmer's cleverness.

Scheherazade finished telling the story of the Clever Farmer and the Mischievous Genie. King Shahryar was impressed by this story and wanted to hear more stories that carry valuable lessons and important morals about intelligence, cunning, and cooperation between humans and genies.

Questions
1. What is the story that Scheherazade began to tell on the sixth night?
2. What did the farmer find in his field?
3. What did the genie think when the farmer released him?
4. What was the plan the farmer had to deal with the genie?
5. How did the life of the farmer and his family improve?

Answers
1. Scheherazade began to tell the story of the Clever Farmer and the Mischievous Genie.
2. The farmer found an old brass vessel buried in his field.
3. The genie thought the farmer would ask for a wish to improve his life.
4. The farmer told the genie that he did not believe in his power and did not think he could return to the vessel. The genie felt angry and humiliated, so he decided to prove his power to the farmer and immediately

returned to the vessel. Once the genie was back in the vessel, the farmer closed the lid with joy.

5. The life of the farmer and his family improved thanks to the genie's power and the farmer's cleverness after the genie promised not to harm anyone and to help the farmer and his family.

الفَصْلُ السّابِعُ
لِصُّ الإِسْكَنْدَرِيَّةِ وَرَئيسُ الشُّرْطَةِ

في إحْدى لَيالي شَهْرَزادَ، بَدَأَتْ تَروي قِصَّةَ لِصِّ الإِسْكَنْدَرِيَّةِ وَرَئيسِ الشُّرْطَةِ.

في مَدينَةِ الإِسْكَنْدَرِيَّةِ الجَميلَةِ، كانَ هُناكَ لِصٌّ ذَكِيٌّ وَماهِرٌ يَسْرِقُ مِنَ الأَغْنِياءِ وَيُوَزِّعُ عَلى الفُقَراءِ. كانَ الجَميعُ يَتَحَدَّثونَ عَنْ هَذا

اللِّصَّ لِأَنَّ أَحَدًا لَمْ يَسْتَطِعِ القَبْضَ عَلَيْهِ. قَرَّرَ رَئِيسُ الشُّرْطَةِ أَنْ يُمْسِكَ بِهَذَا اللِّصَّ وَيَضَعَ حَدًّا لِجَرَائِمِهِ.

فَكَّرَ رَئِيسُ الشُّرْطَةِ في خُطَّةٍ ذَكِيَّةٍ لِإِلْقَاءِ القَبْضِ عَلَى اللِّصِّ. اِنْتَشَرَتْ شَائِعَةٌ عَنْ كَنْزٍ ضَخْمٍ سَيَتِمُّ نَقْلُهُ عَبْرَ المَدِينَةِ. كَانَتْ هَذِهِ الشَّائِعَةُ مُجَرَّدَ فَخٍّ لِجَذْبِ اللِّصِّ.

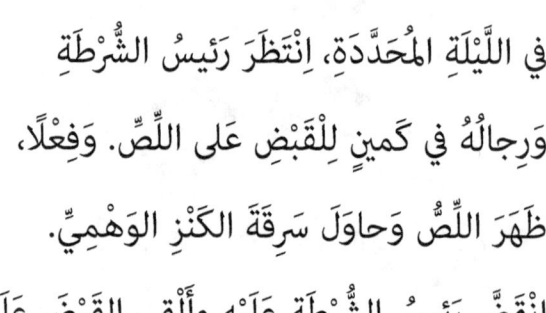

في اللَّيْلَةِ المُحَدَّدَةِ، اِنْتَظَرَ رَئِيسُ الشُّرْطَةِ وَرِجَالُهُ في كَمِينٍ لِلْقَبْضِ عَلَى اللِّصِّ. وَفِعْلًا، ظَهَرَ اللِّصُّ وَحَاوَلَ سَرِقَةَ الكَنْزِ الوَهْمِيِّ. اِنْقَضَّ رَئِيسُ الشُّرْطَةِ عَلَيْهِ وَأَلْقَى القَبْضَ عَلَيْهِ.

لَكِنَّ اللِّصَّ لَمْ يَسْتَسْلِمْ بِسُهُولَةٍ، تَمَكَّنَ مِنَ الهُرُوبِ مِنَ الحِصَارِ وَفَرَّ إِلَى أَحَدِ الأَزِقَّةِ المُظْلِمَةِ. بَدَأَتْ مُطَارَدَةٌ مُثِيرَةٌ بَيْنَ اللِّصِّ وَرَئِيسِ الشُّرْطَةِ في أَنْحَاءِ المَدِينَةِ. في النِّهَايَةِ، اِسْتَطَاعَ رَئِيسُ الشُّرْطَةِ الإِمْسَاكَ بِاللِّصِّ وَأَلْقَى القَبْضَ عَلَيْهِ.

رَغْمَ القَبْضِ عَلَى اللِّصِّ، كَانَ رَئِيسُ الشُّرْطَةِ يَعْتَرِفُ بِذَكاءِ اللِّصِّ وَشَجاعَتِهِ. وَفِي المَحْكَمَةِ، قَرَّرَ القاضي أَنْ يَمْنَحَ اللِّصَّ فُرْصَةً لِتَغْيِيرِ حَياتِهِ بِأَنْ يَعْمَلَ تَحْتَ إِمْرَةِ رَئِيسِ الشُّرْطَةِ لِمُكافَحَةِ الجَرِيمَةِ.

وَهَكَذا انْتَهَتْ قِصَّةُ لِصِّ الإِسْكَنْدَرِيَّةِ وَرَئِيسِ الشُّرْطَةِ، الَّتي عَلَّمَتْنا أَنَّ الذَّكاءَ وَالشَّجاعَةَ يُمْكِنُ اسْتِخْدامُهُما لِلْخَيْرِ.

Questions

1. ماذا كانَ لِصُّ الإِسْكَنْدَرِيَّةِ يَفْعَلُ بَعْدَ سَرِقَتِهِ مِنَ الأَغْنِياءِ؟

2. ماذا قَرَّرَ رَئيسُ الشُّرْطَةِ أَنْ يَفْعَلَ لِلْقَبْضِ عَلى اللِّصِّ؟

3. ماذا حَدَثَ عِنْدَما حاوَلَ اللِّصُّ سَرِقَةَ الكَنْزِ الوَهْمِيِّ؟

4. كَيْفَ اسْتَطاعَ اللِّصُّ الهُروبَ مِنَ الحِصارِ؟

5. ماذا قَرَّرَ القاضي بِخُصوصِ اللِّصِّ بَعْدَ القَبْضِ عَلَيْهِ؟

Answers

1. كانَ لِصُّ الإِسْكَنْدَرِيَّةِ يُوَزِّعُ ما سَرَقَهُ مِنَ الأَغْنِياءِ عَلى الفُقَراءِ.

2. اِسْتَقَرَّ رَئيسُ الشُّرْطَةِ عَلى خُطَّةٍ ذَكِيَّةٍ لِإِلْقاءِ القَبْضِ عَلى اللِّصِّ، وَهِيَ نَشْرُ شائِعَةٍ عَنْ كَنْزٍ ضَخْمٍ سَيَتِمُّ نَقْلُهُ عَبْرَ المَدينَةِ، مُعْتَبِرًا هَذِهِ الشّائِعَةَ فَخًّا لِجَذْبِ اللِّصِّ.

3. عِنْدَما حاوَلَ اللِّصُّ سَرِقَةَ الكَنْزِ الوَهْمِيِّ، اِنْقَضَّ رَئيسُ الشُّرْطَةِ وَرِجالُهُ عَلَيْهِ وأَلْقوا القَبْضَ عَلَيْهِ.

4. اِسْتَطاعَ اللِّصُّ الهُروبَ مِنَ الحِصارِ بِعَدَمِ الاِسْتِسْلامِ بِسُهولَةٍ وَالفِرارِ إلى أَحَدِ الأَزِقَّةِ المُظْلِمَةِ.

5. قَرَّرَ القاضي مَنْحَ اللِّصِّ فُرْصَةً لِتَغْيِيرِ حَياتِهِ بِأَنْ يَعْمَلَ تَحْتَ إِمْرَةِ رَئيسِ الشُّرْطَةِ لِمُكافَحَةِ الجَريمَةِ.

Chapter 7: The Thief of Alexandria and the Police Chief

During one of Shahrazad's nights, she began to tell the story of the Thief of Alexandria and the Police Chief.

In the beautiful city of Alexandria, there was a clever and skilled thief who stole from the rich and gave to the poor. Everyone was talking about this thief because no one could catch him. The police chief decided to catch this thief and put an end to his crimes.

The police chief thought of a clever plan to capture the thief. A rumor spread about a huge treasure that would be transported through the city. This rumor was just a trap to lure the thief.

On the designated night, the police chief and his men waited in ambush to catch the thief. And indeed, the thief appeared and tried to steal the imaginary treasure. The police chief pounced on him and caught him.

But the thief did not surrender easily. He managed to escape the grip and fled into one of the dark alleys. An exciting chase began between the thief and the police chief throughout the city. In the end, the police chief managed to catch the thief and arrested him.

Despite the arrest of the thief, the police chief recognized his intelligence and courage. In court, the judge decided to give the thief a chance to change his life and work under the police chief to fight crime.

And so, the story of the Thief of Alexandria and the Police Chief ended, teaching us that intelligence and courage can be used for good.

Questions
1. What did the Thief of Alexandria do after stealing from the rich?
2. What did the police chief decide to do to catch the thief?
3. What happened when the thief tried to steal the imaginary treasure?
4. How did the thief manage to escape the grip?
5. What did the judge decide about the thief after his arrest?

Answers
1. The Thief of Alexandria distributed what he stole from the rich to the poor.
2. The police chief decided on a clever plan to catch the thief, which was to spread a rumor about a huge treasure that would be transported through the city, considering this rumor a trap to lure the thief.
3. When the thief tried to steal the imaginary treasure, the police chief and his men pounced on him and caught him.

4. The thief managed to escape the grip by not surrendering easily and fleeing into one of the dark alleys.
5. The judge decided to give the thief a chance to change his life and work under the police chief to fight crime.

الفَصْلُ الثّامِنُ
الطّائِرُ الأَزْرَقُ

في اللَّيْلَةِ التّالِيَةِ، بَدَأَتْ شَهْرَزادُ تَرْوي قِصَّةَ الطّائِرِ الأَزْرَقِ لِلْمَلِكِ شَهْرَيارَ.

كانَ هُناكَ طائِرٌ أَزْرَقُ نادِرٌ وَجَميلٌ يَعيشُ في غابَةٍ سِحْرِيَّةٍ بَعيدَةٍ. قيلَ إِنَّ الطّائِرَ الأَزْرَقَ يَمْلِكُ القُدْرَةَ عَلى مَنْحِ السَّعادَةِ وَالحَظِّ

السَّعيدِ لِمَنْ يَتَمَكَّنُ مِنَ العُثورِ عَلَيْهِ. سَمِعَتْ أَميرَةٌ شابَّةٌ عَنِ الطّائِرِ الأَزْرَقِ وَقَرَّرَتِ البَحْثَ عَنْهُ لِتَحْقيقِ السَّعادَةِ لِمَمْلَكَتِها وَشَعْبِها.

انْطَلَقَتِ الأَميرَةُ في رِحْلَةٍ طَويلَةٍ وَمُغامَرَةٍ شَيِّقَةٍ لِلْبَحْثِ عَنِ الطّائِرِ الأَزْرَقِ. تَعَرَّفَتْ خِلالَ رِحْلَتِها عَلى العَديدِ مِنَ الأَصْدِقاءِ وَالحَيَواناتِ المُتَعاوِنَةِ الَّتي ساعَدَتْها في تَجاوُزِ العَقَباتِ وَالمَصاعِبِ.

بَعْدَ سِلْسِلَةٍ طَويلَةٍ مِنَ التَّحَدِّياتِ وَالمُغامَراتِ، تَمَكَّنَتِ الأَميرَةُ مِنَ العُثورِ عَلى الطّائِرِ الأَزْرَقِ. وَلَكِنْ بَدَلًا مِنْ أَنْ يَمْنَحَها السَّعادَةَ مُباشَرَةً، عَلَّمَها الطّائِرُ الأَزْرَقُ أَنَّ السَّعادَةَ الحَقيقِيَّةَ تَأْتي مِنَ العَمَلِ الجادِّ وَالتَّصَدّي لِلْمَشاكِلِ وَالتَّحَدِّياتِ بِشَجاعَةٍ وَعَزيمَةٍ.

عادَتِ الأَميرَةُ إِلى مَمْلَكَتِها وَشارَكَتْ شَعْبَها العِبْرَةَ القَيِّمَةَ الَّتي تَعَلَّمَتْها مِنَ الطّائِرِ الأَزْرَقِ. تَحَسَّنَتْ حَياةُ النّاسِ في المَمْلَكَةِ

وَزادَتْ سَعادَتُهُمْ، وَبِذَلِكَ حَقَّقَتِ الأَميرَةُ هَدَفَها مِنْ خِلالِ العَمَلِ الجادِّ وَالتَّعاوُنِ مَعَ شَعْبِها بَدَلًا مِنَ الِاعْتِمادِ عَلى قُوًى سِحْرِيَّةٍ.

اِنْتَهَتْ شَهْرَزادُ مِنْ سَرْدِ قِصَّةِ الطّائِرِ الأَزْرَقِ. كانَ المَلِكُ شَهْرَيارُ مَذهولًا بِالقِصَّةِ وَأَرادَ سَماعَ المَزيدِ مِنَ القِصَصِ الَّتي تَحْمِلُ دُروسًا قَيِّمَةً وَعِبَرًا هامَّةً. وَبِهَذا الشَّكْلِ، اِسْتَمَرَّتْ شَهْرَزادُ في سَرْدِ قِصَصِها لِلْمَلِكِ شَهْرَيارَ لَيْلَةً بَعْدَ لَيْلَةٍ، مُعَلِّمَةً إيّاهُ وَشَعْبَهُ دُروسًا هامَّةً عَنِ العَمَلِ الجادِّ وَالتَّصَدّي لِلتَّحَدِّياتِ بِشَجاعَةٍ وَعَزيمَةٍ.

Questions

1. ما هِيَ القِصَّةُ الَّتي بَدَأَتْ شَهْرَزادُ تَرْويها في اللَّيْلَةِ الثَّامِنَةِ؟

2. ما هِيَ القُدْرَةُ السِّحْرِيَّةُ الَّتي يَمْلِكُها الطَّائِرُ الأَزْرَقُ؟

3. لِماذا قَرَّرَتِ الأَميرَةُ البَحْثَ عَنِ الطَّائِرِ الأَزْرَقِ؟

4. ما العِبْرَةُ القَيِّمَةُ الَّتي تَعَلَّمَتْها الأَميرَةُ مِنَ الطَّائِرِ الأَزْرَقِ؟

5. كَيْفَ تَحَسَّنَتْ حَياةُ النّاسِ في المَمْلَكَةِ بَعْدَ عَوْدَةِ الأَميرَةِ؟

Answers

1. بَدَأَتْ شَهْرَزادُ تَرْوي قِصَّةَ الطّائِرِ الأَزْرَقِ.

2. يَمْلِكُ الطّائِرُ الأَزْرَقُ القُدْرَةَ عَلى مَنْحِ السَّعادَةِ وَالحَظِّ السَّعيدِ لِمَنْ يَتَمَكَّنُ مِنَ العُثورِ عَلَيْهِ.

3. قَرَّرَتِ الأَميرَةُ البَحْثَ عَنِ الطّائِرِ الأَزْرَقِ لِتَحْقيقِ السَّعادَةِ لِمَمْلَكَتِها وَشَعْبِها.

4. تَعَلَّمَتِ الأَميرَةُ مِنَ الطّائِرِ الأَزْرَقِ أَنَّ السَّعادَةَ الحَقيقِيَّةَ تَأْتي مِنَ العَمَلِ الجادِّ وَالتَّصَدّي لِلْمَشاكِلِ وَالتَّحَدّياتِ بِشَجاعَةٍ وَعَزيمَةٍ.

5. تَحَسَّنَتْ حَياةُ النّاسِ في المَمْلَكَةِ وَزادَتْ سَعادَتُهُمْ بَعْدَ أَنْ شارَكَتِ الأَميرَةُ شَعْبَها العِبْرَةَ القَيِّمَةَ الَّتي تَعَلَّمَتْها مِنَ الطّائِرِ الأَزْرَقِ وَحَقَّقَتْ هَدَفَها مِنْ خِلالِ العَمَلِ الجادِّ وَالتَّعاوُنِ مَعَ شَعْبِها بَدَلًا مِنَ الِاعْتِمادِ عَلى قُوًى سِحْرِيَّةٍ.

Chapter 8: The Blue Bird

On the following night, Scheherazade began telling the story of the Blue Bird to King Shahryar.

There was a rare and beautiful blue bird that lived in a distant magical forest. It was said that the blue bird had the ability to grant happiness and good luck to those who could find it. A young princess heard about the Blue Bird and decided to search for it to bring happiness to her kingdom and its people.

The princess embarked on a long and exciting adventure to find the Blue Bird. She met, on her journey, many friends and helpful animals who helped her overcome obstacles and challenges.

After a long series of challenges and adventures, the princess finally found the Blue Bird. But instead of giving her happiness directly, the Blue Bird taught her that true happiness comes from hard work and facing problems and challenges with courage and determination.

The princess returned to her kingdom and shared the valuable lesson she learned from the Blue Bird with her people. Their lives improved, and their happiness increased. The princess had achieved her goal through hard work and cooperation with her people instead of relying on magical powers.

Scheherazade finished telling the story of the Blue Bird. King Shahryar was amazed by the story and wanted to hear more stories that carry valuable lessons and important morals. And so, Scheherazade continued to tell her stories to King Shahryar night after night, teaching him and his people important lessons about hard work and facing challenges with courage and determination.

Questions
1. What story did Scheherazade begin telling on the eighth night?
2. What magical ability does the Blue Bird have?
3. Why did the princess decide to search for the Blue Bird?
4. What valuable lesson did the princess learn from the Blue Bird?
5. How did people's lives improve in the kingdom after the princess's return?

Answers
1. Scheherazade began telling the story of the Blue Bird.
2. The Blue Bird has the ability to grant happiness and good luck to those who can find it.
3. The princess decided to search for the Blue Bird to bring happiness to her kingdom and its people.
4. The princess learned from the Blue Bird that true happiness comes from hard work and facing problems and challenges with courage and determination.

5. People's lives in the kingdom improved, and their happiness increased after the princess shared the valuable lesson she learned from the Blue Bird and achieved her goal through hard work and cooperation with her people instead of relying on magical powers.

الفَصْلُ التّاسِعُ
الفَتاةُ وَالعَجوزُ السِّحْرِيَّةُ

في اللَّيْلَةِ التّالِيَةِ، بَدَأَتْ شَهْرَزادُ تَرْوي قِصَّةَ الفَتاةِ وَالعَجوزِ السِّحْرِيَّةِ لِلْمَلِكِ شَهْرَيارَ.

كانَتْ هُناكَ فَتاةٌ شابَّةٌ تَعيشُ مَعَ والِدَتِها في قَرْيَةٍ صَغيرَةٍ. كانَتِ الفَتاةُ تُعاني مِنَ الفَقْرِ وَالجوعِ. في يَوْمٍ مِنَ الأَيّامِ، وَجَدَتْ عَجوزًا

تَبيعُ الوُرودَ في السّوقِ. اِشْتَرَتِ الفَتاةُ وَرْدَةً مِنَ العَجوزِ بِما لَدَيْها مِنْ مالٍ قَليلٍ.

اِبْتَسَمَتِ العَجوزُ وَشَكَرَتِ الفَتاةَ عَلى لُطْفِها. كَشَفَتِ العَجوزُ أَنَّها ساحِرَةٌ وَعَرَضَتْ عَلى الفَتاةِ أَنْ تُحَقِّقَ لَها أُمْنِيَّةً واحِدَةً. فَكَّرَتِ الفَتاةُ في ما تُريدُهُ وَقَرَّرَتْ أَنْ تَطْلُبَ مِنَ العَجوزِ السِّحْرِيَّةِ أَنْ تَمْنَحَها القُدْرَةَ عَلى إِسْعادِ النّاسِ مِنْ حَوْلِها.

مَنَحَتِ العَجوزُ السِّحْرِيَّةُ الفَتاةَ الهِبَةَ الَّتي طَلَبَتْها. بَدَأَتِ الفَتاةُ في اسْتِخْدامِ هَذِهِ القُدْرَةِ لِإِسْعادِ النّاسِ في قَرْيَتِها. مَعَ مُرورِ الوَقْتِ، اِنْتَشَرَتْ شُهْرَةُ الفَتاةِ وَأَصْبَحَتْ مَحْبوبَةً وَمُقَدَّرَةً مِنَ الجَميعِ.

اِنْتَهَتْ شَهْرَزادُ مِنْ سَرْدِ قِصَّةِ الفَتاةِ وَالعَجوزِ السِّحْرِيَّةِ. كانَ المَلِكُ شَهْرَيارُ مُعْجَبًا بِهَذِهِ القِصَّةِ وَأَرادَ سَماعَ القِصَصِ الَّتي تَحْمِلُ دُروسًا قَيِّمَةً وَعِبَرًا هامَّةً عَنِ الإِحْسانِ وَالتَّفاني لِخِدْمَةِ الآخَرينَ. وَبِهَذا الشَّكْلِ، اِسْتَمَرَّتْ شَهْرَزادُ

في سَرْدِ قِصَصِها لِلْمَلِكِ شَهْرَيارَ لَيْلَةً بَعْدَ لَيْلَةٍ، مُعَلِّمَةً إيّاهُ وَشَعْبَهُ دُروسًا هامَّةً عَنِ الإيثارِ وَالتَّفاني لِمُساعَدَةِ النّاسِ وَتَحْقيقِ السَّعادَةِ لِلْجَميعِ.

Questions

1. ما هِيَ القِصَّةُ الَّتي بَدَأَتْ شَهْرَزادُ تَرويها في اللَّيْلَةِ التّاسِعَةِ؟

2. ماذا كانَتِ العَجوزُ تَبيعُ في السّوقِ؟

3. ماذا طَلَبَتِ الفَتاةُ مِنَ العَجوزِ السِّحْرِيَّةِ؟

4. كَيْفَ أَثَّرَتِ الهِبَةُ الَّتي مَنَحَتْها العَجوزُ السِّحْرِيَّةُ لِلْفَتاةِ عَلى حَياتِها؟

5. ما هِيَ الدُّروسُ الهامَّةُ الَّتي عَلَّمَتها شَهْرَزادُ لِلْمَلِكِ شَهْرَيارَ وَشَعْبِهِ مِنْ خِلالِ هَذِهِ القِصَّةِ؟

Answers

١. بَدَأَتْ شَهْرَزادُ تَرْوي قِصَّةَ الفَتاةِ وَالعَجوزِ السِّحْرِيَّةِ.

٢. كانَتِ العَجوزُ تَبيعُ الوُرودَ في السّوقِ.

٣. طَلَبَتِ الفَتاةُ مِنَ العَجوزِ السِّحْرِيَّةِ أَنْ تَمْنَحَها القُدْرَةَ عَلى إِسْعادِ النّاسِ مِنْ حَوْلِها.

٤. بَدَأَتِ الفَتاةُ في اسْتِخْدامِ هَذِهِ القُدْرَةِ لِإِسْعادِ النّاسِ في قَرْيَتِها، وَمَعَ مُرورِ الوَقْتِ انْتَشَرَتْ شُهْرَةُ الفَتاةِ وَأَصْبَحَتْ مَحْبوبَةً وَمُقَدَّرَةً مِنَ الجَميعِ.

٥. عَلَّمَتْ شَهْرَزادُ المَلِكَ شَهْرْيارَ وَشَعْبَهُ دُروسًا هامَّةً عَنِ الإيثارِ وَالتَّفاني لِمُساعَدَةِ النّاسِ وَتَحْقيقِ السَّعادَةِ لِلْجَميعِ.

Chapter 9: The Girl and the Magical Old Woman

On the following night, Scheherazade began telling the story of the Girl and the Magical Old Woman to King Shahryar.

There was a young girl who lived with her mother in a small village. The girl suffered from poverty and hunger. One day, she stumbled upon an old woman selling flowers in the market. The girl bought a flower from the old woman with the little money she had.

The old woman smiled and thanked the girl for her kindness. She revealed that she was a sorceress and offered to grant the girl one wish. The girl thought about what she wanted and decided to ask the magical old woman to give her the ability to make people around her happy.

The magical old woman granted the girl the gift she asked for. The girl began using this ability to make people in her village happy. With time, the girl's fame spread, and she became beloved and honored by everyone.

Scheherazade finished telling the story of the Girl and the Magical Old Woman. King Shahryar was impressed by this story and wanted to hear stories that carried valuable lessons and important morals about kindness and dedication to serving others. And so, Scheherazade continued to tell her stories to King Shahryar night after night, teaching him and his people important lessons about generosity and selflessness to help others and achieve happiness for all.

Questions
1. What story did Scheherazade start telling on the ninth night?
2. What was the old woman selling in the market?
3. What did the girl ask the magical old woman for?
4. How did the gift given to the girl by the magical old woman affect her life?
5. What important lessons did Scheherazade teach King Shahryar and his people through this story?

Answers
1. Scheherazade started telling the story of the girl and the magical old woman.
2. The old woman was selling flowers in the market.
3. The girl asked the magical old woman to grant her the ability to make people around her happy.
4. The girl began using this ability to make people happy in her village, and over time, her fame spread, and she became loved and honored by everyone.
5. Scheherazade taught King Shahryar and his people important lessons about sacrifice and selflessness in helping others and achieving happiness for all.

الفَصْلُ العاشِرُ
الأَميرُ وَالتِّنينُ

في اللَّيْلَةِ التّاليَةِ، بَدَأَتْ شَهْرَزادُ تَرْوي قِصَّةَ الأَميرِ وَالتِّنّينِ لِلْمَلِكِ شَهْرَيارَ.

كانَ هُناكَ أَميرٌ شابٌ وَشُجاعٌ يَعيشُ في مَمْلَكَةٍ بَعيدَةٍ. انْتَشَرَ في البِلادِ خَبَرٌ عَنْ تِنّينٍ ضَخْمٍ يَعيشُ في جَبَلٍ قَريبٍ، يُهَدِّدُ القُرى

المُجاوِرَة وَيُخيفُ النّاسَ. قَرَّرَ الأَميرُ أَنْ يُواجِهَ التِّنّينَ وَيُنقِذَ شَعبَهُ مِنَ الخَطَرِ.

اِستَعَدَّ الأَميرُ لِلمَعرَكَةِ وَتَوَجَّهَ إِلى الجَبَلِ. عِندَما واجَهَ الأَميرُ التِّنّينَ، اِكتَشَفَ أَنَّهُ لَيسَ شِرّيرًا كَما اعتَقَدَ الجَميعُ. بَلْ كانَ يُسَبِّبُ الدَّمارَ بِسَبَبِ أَلَمٍ يُعاني مِنهُ في جَسَدِهِ. عَرَضَ الأَميرُ أَنْ يُساعِدَ التِّنّينَ لِعِلاجِ أَلَمِهِ مُقابِلَ وَعدٍ بِعَدَمِ إِلحاقِ الأَذى بِالنّاسِ مَرَّةً أُخرى.

وافَقَ التِّنّينُ عَلى الاتِّفاقِ وَقامَ الأَميرُ بِمُساعَدَتِهِ. بَعدَ شِفاءِ التِّنّينِ، عاشَ هُوَ وَالأَميرُ في سَلامٍ وَصَداقَةٍ، وَتَعاوَنا لِحِمايَةِ القُرى وَالبِلادِ مِنَ الأَعداءِ وَالمَخاطِرِ.

اِنتَهَتْ شَهرَزادُ مِنْ سَردِ قِصَّةِ الأَميرِ وَالتِّنّينِ. كانَ المَلِكُ شَهرَيارُ مُعجَبًا بِهَذِهِ القِصَّةِ وَأَرادَ سَماعَ المَزيدِ مِنَ القِصَصِ الَّتي تَحمِلُ دُروسًا قَيِّمَةً وَعِبَرًا هامَّةً عَنِ الصَّداقَةِ وَالتَّفاهُمِ بَينَ الكائِناتِ المُختَلِفَةِ.

وَبِهَذا الشَّكْلِ، اِسْتَمَرَّتْ شَهْرَزادُ في سَرْدِ قِصَصِها المَلِيئَةِ بِالْعِبَرِ وَالحِكَمِ لِلْمَلِكِ شَهْرَيارَ كُلَّ لَيْلَةٍ. تَأَثَّرَ المَلِكُ شَهْرَيارُ بِشَكْلٍ عَمِيقٍ بِكَلِماتِ شَهْرَزادَ وَعِبَرِها القَيِّمَةِ، وَتَغَيَّرَتْ نَظْرَتُهُ لِلْحَياةِ وَالعالَمِ مِنْ حَوْلِهِ.

بِفَضْلِ حِكْمَةِ شَهْرَزادَ وَقُدْرَتِها عَلَى التَّواصُلِ وَنَقْلِ العِبَرِ وَالدُّروسِ القَيِّمَةِ مِنْ خِلالِ قِصَصِها، أَصْبَحَ المَلِكُ شَهْرَيارُ مَلِكًا حَكِيمًا وَعادِلًا. أَعادَ السَّلامَ وَالاِزْدِهارَ إِلَى مَمْلَكَتِهِ وَحَكَمَ بِحِكْمَةٍ وَرَحْمَةٍ لَمْ يَشْهَدْها الشَّعْبُ مِنْ قَبْلُ.

مَعَ مُرورِ الوَقْتِ، أَدْرَكَ المَلِكُ شَهْرَيارُ أَنَّهُ وَجَدَ في شَهْرَزادَ زَوْجَةً حَكِيمَةً وَمُخْلِصَةً. أَصْبَحَتْ شَهْرَزادُ مَلِكَةً مَحْبوبَةً مِنَ الشَّعْبِ وَأَمًّا لِلْأَميرَةِ الصَّغيرَةِ.

واصَلَتْ شَهْرَزادُ سَرْدَ القِصَصِ لِلْمَلِكِ كُلَّ لَيْلَةٍ، مِمَّا جَعَلَهُ يُقَدِّرُها وَيَحْتَرِمُها أَكْثَرَ فَأَكْثَرَ. وَعاشَ المَلِكُ شَهْرَيارُ وَشَهْرَزادُ سَعيدَيْنِ مَعًا، حَيْثُ اسْتَمَرَّتْ قِصَصُها في نَشْرِ الحِكْمَةِ وَالمَعْرِفَةِ في كُلِّ أَرْجاءِ المَمْلَكَةِ.

وَبِهَذِهِ الطَّرِيقَةِ، اِسْتَمَرَّتْ شَهْرَزادُ في نَسْجِ القِصَصِ المُثيرَةِ وَالرّائِعَةِ لِلْمَلِكِ شَهْرَيارَ لَيْلَةً بَعْدَ لَيْلَةٍ، مَعَ تَعَلُّمِها وتَعَلُّمِهِ مِنْ دُروسِها وَعَجائِبِها. وَظَلَّتِ المَمْلَكَةُ تَزْدَهِرُ تَحْتَ حِكْمَةِ وَسَعادَةِ شَهْرَزاد وَشَهْرَيارَ، بَيْنَما أَلْهَمَتْ قِصَصُ لَيالي الأَلْفِ لَيْلَةٍ وَلَيْلَةٍ النّاسَ في جَميعِ أَنْحاءِ العالَمِ.

Questions

1. ما هِيَ القِصَّةُ الَّتي بَدَأَتْ شَهْرَزادُ تَرْويها في اللَّيْلَةِ العاشِرَةِ؟

2. ما الخَبَرُ الَّذي انْتَشَرَ عَنِ التِّنِّينِ الَّذي يَعيشُ في الجَبَلِ؟

3. ماذا اكْتَشَفَ الأَميرُ عِنْدَما واجَهَ التِّنِّينَ؟

4. ما هُوَ الاِتِّفاقُ الَّذي قَطَعَهُ الأَميرُ مَعَ التِّنِّينِ؟

5. كَيْفَ أَثَّرَتْ قِصَصُ شَهْرَزادَ عَلى المَلِكِ شَهْرَيارَ وَمَمْلَكَتِهِ؟

Answers

1. بَدَأَتْ شَهْرَزادُ تَروي قِصَّةَ الأميرِ وَالتِّنّينِ.

2. اِنْتَشَرَ خَبَرٌ عَنْ تِنّينٍ ضَخْمٍ يَعيشُ في جَبَلٍ قَريبٍ، يُهَدِّدُ القُرى المُجاوِرَةَ وَيُخيفُ النّاسَ.

3. اِكْتَشَفَ الأميرُ أَنَّ التِّنّينَ لَيْسَ شِرّيرًا كَما اعْتَقَدَ الجَميعُ، بَلْ كانَ يُسَبِّبُ الدَّمارَ بِسَبَبِ أَلَمٍ يُعاني مِنْهُ في جَسَدِهِ.

4. عَرَضَ الأميرُ أَنْ يُساعِدَ التِّنّينَ لِعِلاجِ أَلَمِهِ مُقابِلَ وَعَدٍ بِعَدَمِ إِلْحاقِ الأَذى بِالنّاسِ مَرَّةً أُخْرى، وَوافَقَ التِّنّينُ عَلى الاِتِّفاقِ.

5. تَأَثَّرَ المَلِكُ شَهْرَيارُ بِشَكْلٍ عَميقٍ بِكَلِماتِ شَهْرَزادَ وَعِبَرِها القَيِّمَةِ، وَتَغَيَّرَتْ نَظْرَتُهُ لِلْحَياةِ وَالعالَمِ مِنْ حَوْلِهِ. أَصْبَحَ مَلِكًا حَكيمًا وَعادِلًا وَأَعادَ السَّلامَ وَالاِزْدِهارَ إِلى مَمْلَكَتِهِ. تَعَلَّمَ شَعْبُهُ مِنَ العِبَرِ وَالدُّروسِ القَيِّمَةِ الَّتي تَحْمِلُها قِصَصُ شَهْرَزادَ، وَازْدَهَرَتِ المَمْلَكَةُ وَعاشَ شَعْبُها في سَلامٍ وَسَعادَةٍ.

Chapter 10: The Prince and the Dragon

On the next night, Scheherazade began telling the story of the Prince and the Dragon to King Shahryar.

There was a young and brave prince who lived in a distant kingdom. News spread in the land about a huge dragon living in a nearby mountain, threatening the neighboring villages and scaring people. The prince decided to face the dragon and save his people from danger.

The prince prepared for the battle and headed to the mountain. When he faced the dragon, he discovered that the dragon was not evil as everyone thought. Rather, he caused destruction because of pain in his body. The prince offered to help the dragon to heal his pain in exchange for a promise not to harm people again.

The dragon agreed to the deal, and the prince helped him. After the dragon healed, the prince and the dragon lived in peace and friendship, and they cooperated to protect the villages and the country from enemies and risks.

Scheherazade finished narrating the story of the Prince and the Dragon. King Shahryar was impressed by this story and wanted to hear more stories that carry valuable lessons and important messages about friendship and understanding between different creatures.

And so, Scheherazade continued to tell her stories filled with lessons and wisdom to King Shahryar every night. King Shahryar was deeply affected by Scheherazade's words and valuable messages, and his view of life and the world around him changed.

Thanks to Scheherazade's wisdom and her ability to communicate and convey valuable lessons and messages through her stories, King Shahryar became a wise and just king. He restored peace and prosperity to his kingdom and ruled with wisdom and mercy that the people had not seen before.

Over time, King Shahriyar realized that he had found in Scheherazade a wise and loyal wife. Scheherazade became a beloved queen to the people and a mother to the little princess.

Scheherazade continued to tell stories to the king every night, making him appreciate and respect her more and more. King Shahriyar and Scheherazade lived happily together as her stories continued to spread wisdom and knowledge throughout the kingdom.

And thus, Scheherazade continued to weave her thrilling and wonderful stories for King Shahriyar night after night, learning from them and teaching him with her lessons and marvels. The kingdom thrived under the wisdom and happiness of Scheherazade and Shahriyar, while the tales of One Thousand and One Nights inspired people all over the world.

Questions

1. What was the story that Scheherazade began telling on the tenth night?
2. What rumor spread about the dragon living in the mountain?
3. What did the prince discover when he faced the dragon?
4. What agreement did the prince make with the dragon?
5. How did Scheherazade's stories affect King Shahryar and his kingdom?

Answers

1. Scheherazade began telling the story of the Prince and the Dragon.
2. Rumors spread in the land about a huge dragon living in a nearby mountain, threatening the neighboring villages and scaring people.
3. The prince discovered that the dragon was not evil as everyone thought. Rather, he caused destruction because of pain in his body.
4. The prince offered to help the dragon to heal his pain in exchange for a promise not to harm people again, and the dragon agreed to the agreement.
5. King Shahryar was deeply affected by Scheherazade's words and valuable messages, and his view of life and the world around him changed. He became a wise and just king who restored peace and prosperity to his

kingdom. The people learned from the lessons and valuable messages carried by Scheherazade's stories, and the kingdom prospered, and its people lived in peace and happiness.

lingualism

Visit our website for information on current and upcoming titles and free language learning resources.

www.lingualism.com

www.ingramcontent.com/pod-product-compliance
Lightning Source LLC
Chambersburg PA
CBHW062035120526
44592CB00036B/2145